JIM BRICKMAN
Christmas Themes
FOR SOLO PIANO

Project Manager: Jeannette DeLisa
Book Design: Odalis Soto
Transcribed by: David Pugh

Contents

Joy To The World

TRADITIONAL

C
G5
C(9)
C
Dm7
C/E
F(9)
G
C
mf
Fmaj7
G
C(9)
C
Dm7
C/E
C
Dm7
Cmaj7/E
C
C/E
G

G7sus
Am
F
C
G7
Am
Fmaj7
Em7
Dm7
Dm7/G
C
Dm7
Cmaj7/E
F
G
C
Fmaj7
G(9)
C(9)
C
Dm7
C/E

C
Dm7
Cmaj7/E
C
Dm7
C/E
G
G7
Am
F
C
G
C
Am
F
C
G7
Am
Fmaj7

F(9)
Cmaj7/E
Dm7
Dm7/G
C(9)
F
G7
C(9)
C
Dm7
C/E
C
Dm7
Cmaj7/E
F(9)
G7
Am
F
C
G
C
poco rit.
Broadly
Am
F(9)
C
C/G
G7
C
mp
rit. e dim.
p

Silent Night

Words and Music by
FRANZ GRUBER and JOSEPH MOHR

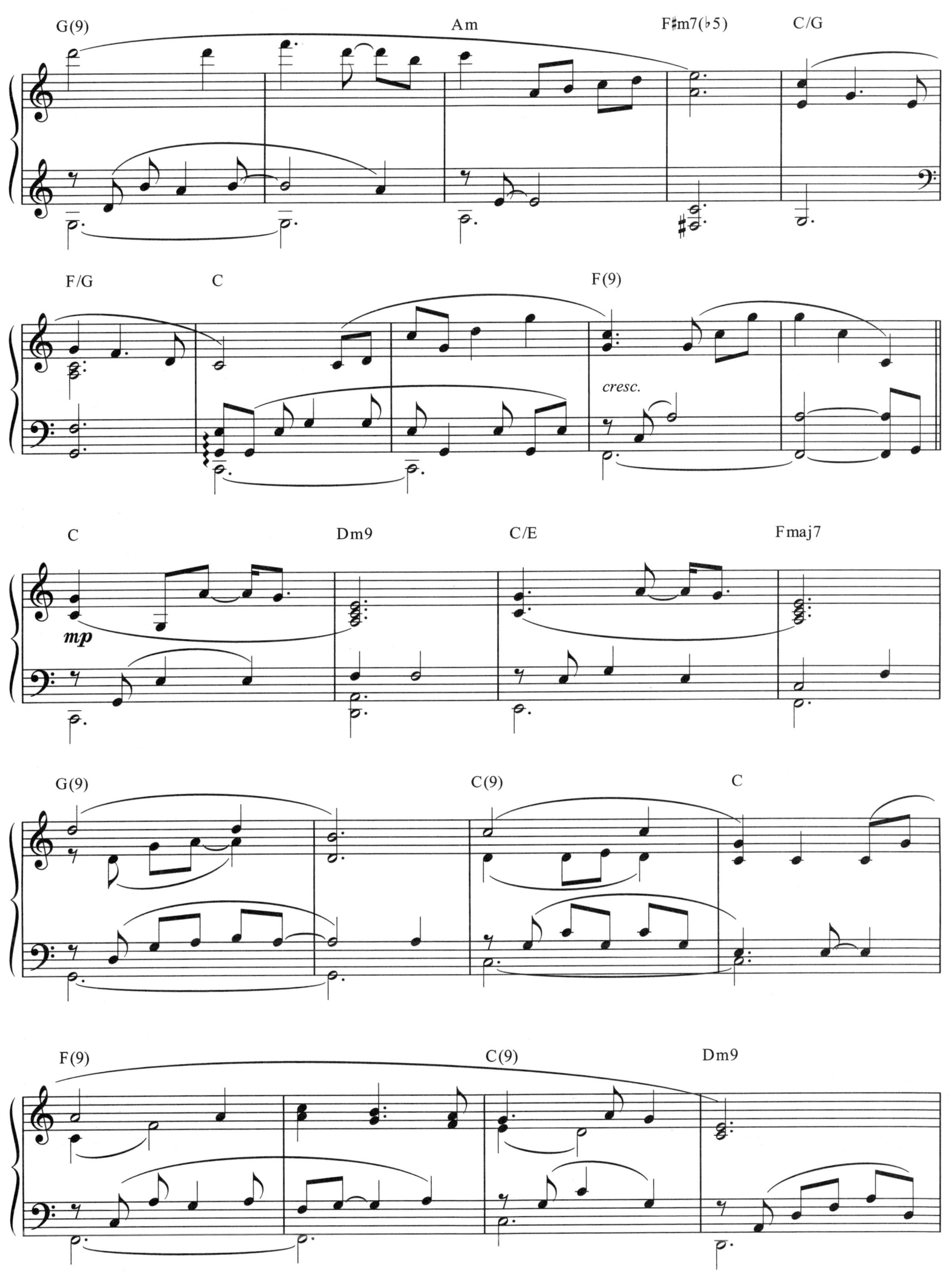
G(9)
Am
F♯m7(♭5)
C/G
F/G
C
F(9)
cresc.
C
Dm9
C/E
Fmaj7
mp
G(9)
C(9)
C
F(9)
C(9)
Dm9

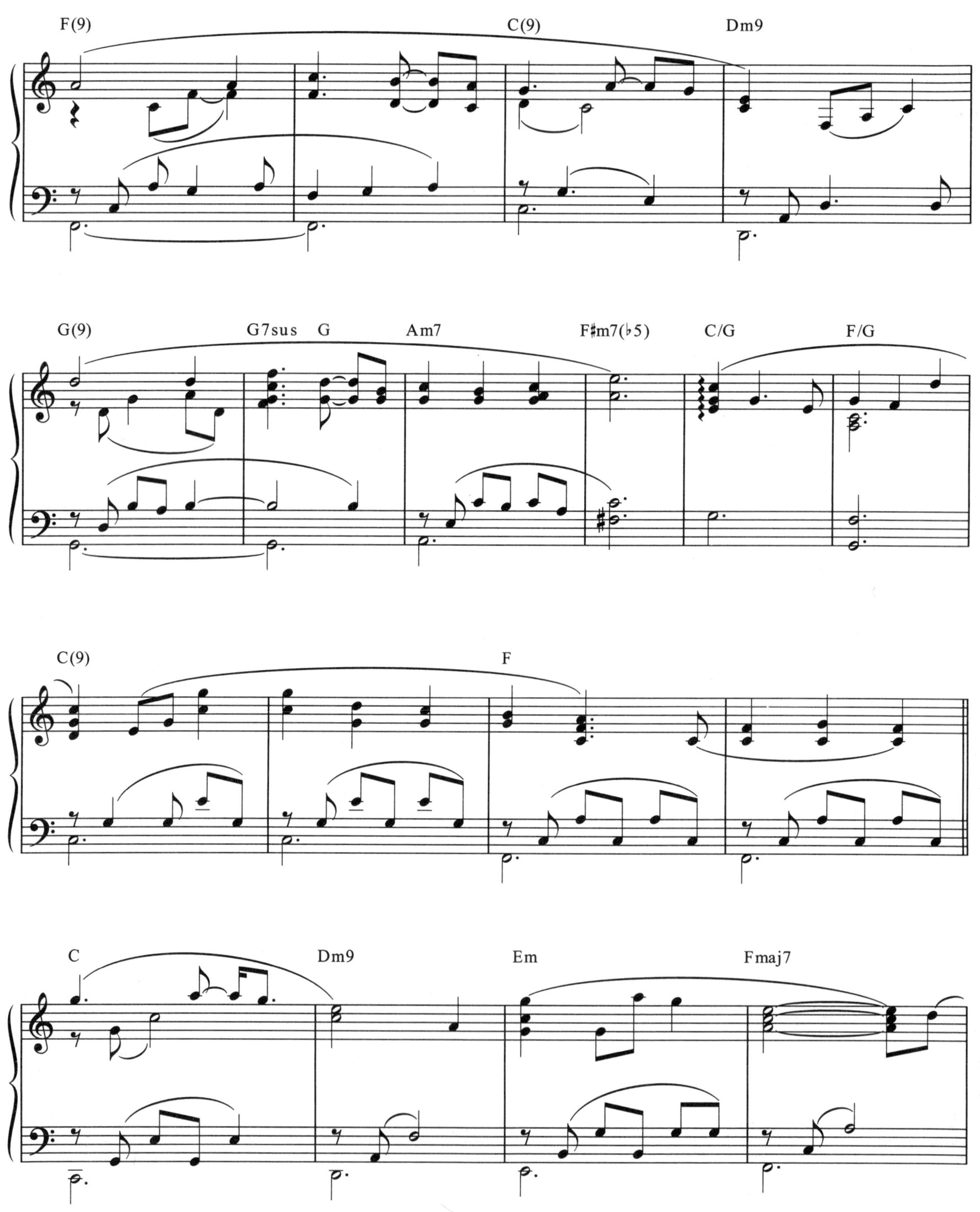
F(9)
C(9)
Dm9
G(9)
G7sus G
Am7
F♯m7(♭5)
C/G
F/G
C(9)
F
C
Dm9
Em
Fmaj7

G
C(9)
F
C
Dm9
F
C
Dm9
G
dim.
G7
Am7
F♯m7(♭5)
C/G
G7sus
C(9)
p rit. e dim.
pp

Have Yourself A Merry Little Christmas

Words and Music by
HUGH MARTIN and RALPH BLANE

F♯m7(♭5)
B7(♭9)
Em
Dsus
G7sus
G7
C(9)
Am7
F(9)
G
C
Am7
F(9)
G
C(9)
Am7
Dm
E7
Am(9)
Am
Am7
C7sus
dim.
Fmaj7
Am
Dm7
G7
Am(9)
D/F♯
p
Fmaj7
Dm7
G7
C(9)
Am7
F(9)
G
C(9)
rit. e dim.
pp

Do You Hear What I Hear?

Words and Music by
NOEL REGNEY and GLORIA SHAYNE

Em
F
G
C(9)
G/B
Am
Am/G
F
G7
Csus
C
cresc.
mp
F
Gsus
C
C
C2
C
Am
Em
F
G
C
G/B
Am
G
F
G7
Em
F(9)

F
G7
Csus
C
Am
Em
F
G
A(9)
dim.
p
Fmaj7
G7sus
G7
C
Csus
C
C
F
Gsus
cresc.
mp
C
Csus/G
C
C2
C
Am(9)
Em7
F
G
dim.
p
cresc.

C G/B Am Em/G F G7sus G7 Em F(9)
mp
F G7 F(9) C/E Dm7 G7sus
C C2 C C2 Am7 F G7
Dm7(4) Dm7 C/E F G7sus G7 C F6 9
rit. e dim.
p
C F(9) C(9)
8va
pp

Silver Bells

Words and Music by
JAY LIVINGSTON and RAY EVANS

C
Csus
C
F
F(9)
mp
G
Dm7/G
C(9)
F/G
C
Csus
C
F
F(9)
G
Dm7/G
C(9)
F
G
cresc.

C(9)
Dm9
F(9)
F
mf
G
Dm7/G
Csus
C
Dm7/G
C(9)
Dm9
F(9)
G
F/G
C(9)
C
F(9)
G
G7
C(9)
Dm7
Em7
F
G/F
F(9)

G(9)
Dm7/G
C(9)
G
C(9)
F
G/F
F(9)
dim.
G
Dm7/G
Am(9)
mp
F(9)
G
cresc.
C
Dm7
C/E
F
F(9)
F
mf

G
Dm7/G
G
C(9)
Dm7/G
C
Dm7
C/E
F
G/F
F(9)
G
Dm7/G
G7
Am(9)
D/F♯
F(9)
G(9)
dim.
mp
C
F(9)
C
rit. e dim.
p

OTHER WINDHAM HILL RELEASES BY OR FEATURING

JIM BRICKMAN

INCLUDE:

NO WORDS • PIANO SAMPLER 2 • A WINTER SOLSTICE V
WINDHAM HILL SAMPLER 1996 • BY HEART • THE CAROLS OF CHRISTMAS

JIM BRICKMAN would like to invite you to be on his Mailing List to receive information about concert schedules, merchandise and upcoming releases. Please fill out the coupon below and mail to:

JIM BRICKMAN
c/o EDGE MANAGEMENT
11288 VENTURA BLVD. SUITE 606
STUDIO CITY, CA 91604

(818) 508-8400 **phone**
(818) 508-8444 **fax**

or

E-Mail us at BrickPiano@AOL.com.
Also, please visit our current Internet Site on the Worldwide Web at WINDHAM.com.

Cut Along Here ✂

NAME ______________________

ADDRESS ______________________

CITY __________ **STATE** __________ **ZIP** __________

SEX: **M**___ **F**___ **E-Mail** ______________________

I first heard about Jim Brickman's music ______________________

Christmas Themes for Solo Piano